I Know God

**written and illustrated
by Dan Foote**

FaithKidz®
Equipping Kids for Life

An Imprint of Cook Communications Ministries
Colorado Springs, CO

Faith Parenting Guide
Ages 4-7
Faith

A Faith Parenting Guide
can be found on page 32.

Additional copies of this book are available from your local bookstore.

If you have enjoyed this book, or if it has impacted your life,
we would like to hear from you.

Please contact us at:
Cook Communications Ministries
4050 Lee Vance View
Colorado Springs, CO 80918
www.cookministries.com

Faith Kidz is an imprint of Cook Communications Ministries
Colorado Springs, Colorado 80918
Cook Communications, Paris, Ontario
Kingsway Communications, Eastbourne, England

First printing, 2005
Manufactured in China.
1 2 3 4 5 6 7 8 9 10 Printing/Year 08 07 06 05

ISBN 078144103X

Editor: Heather Gemmen
Creative Director: Randy Maid
Design Manager: Nancy L. Haskins
Cover Designer: Helen Harrison/YaYe Design
Interior Designer: Patricia Keene

DEDICATION

**To Tom Brunsman—
I know God made me and made you
Best friends since we were two
A "friend who sticks closer than a brother."**

**Through the good times and bad
I've always known I had
A touchstone, a comrade like no other.**

I know God.

I know God
made the sky, the trees,
the big bumblebees,
and the hill where the cow likes to rest.

He made grass, the breeze,
and Grandma's sweet peas.
He colored the robin's red breast.

These are just some
of the things he has done
that make me shout out,
"I know God!"

I know God
made the fish and the frogs,
their small polliwogs,
and the beaver who lives by the lake.

He made the turtle and toad
who are crossing the road
to escape from the slimy green snake.

These are just some
of the things he has done
that make me shout out,
"I know God!"

I know God
made the calf in the stall
trying hard not to fall
as it wobbles and struggles to eat.

He made the kitten and pup
drinking up from the cup
and all of their breath so sweet.

These are just some
of the things he has done
that make me shout out,
"I know God!"

11

I know God
made the owl, the 'coon,
the big, bright full moon,
and fireflies to light up the night.

He gave crickets their tune
in the middle of June
to sing of this wonderful sight.

These are just some
of the things he has done
that make me shout out,
"I know God!"

I know God
made the trees orange and brown
with their leaves falling down
and pumpkins the size of Vermont.

He made cider and grapes
and fruit of all shapes
and a harvest of all that you'd want.

These are just some
of the things he has done
that make me shout out,
"I know God!"

I know God
made the snow and the pines,
the ice on the lines,
and the frost that covers the glass.

He made cocoa and tea
to drink after we ski
and the warmth of the fire's soft glow.

These are just some
of the things he has done
that make me shout out,
"I know God!"

17

Silent Night... Holy Night...

18

I know God
made a star in the sky
shining on high
and wise men with presents to bring.

He told angels to fly
to shepherds nearby
announcing that Jesus is King.

These are just some
of the things he has done
that make me shout out,
"I know God!"

I know God
made the clouds and the rain
swirling fast down the drain
and puddles to walk through and splash.

He made the big gale
and even the hail
and thunder that booms with a CRASH!

These are just some
of the things he has done
that make me shout out,
"I know God!"

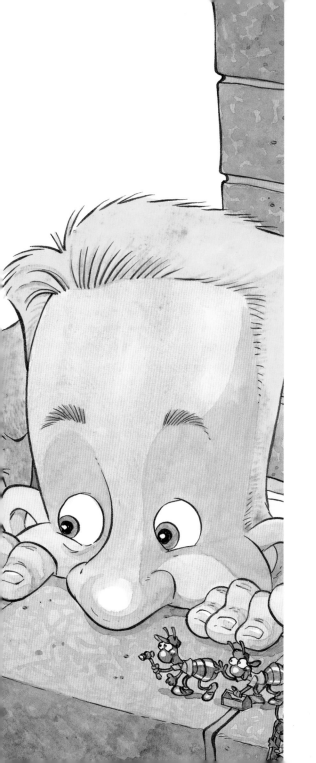

I know God
made the caterpillar crawl
over the wall
to give its cocoon a fair try.

He made it spin like a song
and then before long
out comes a new butterfly.

These are just some
of the things he has done
that make me shout out,
"I know God!"

I know God
made the sun and the stars,
Jupiter and Mars,
and all of the stuff out in space.

He made Saturn's rings...
among other things—
like the craters that cover Moon's face.

These are just some
of the things he has done
that make me shout out,
"I know God!"

I know God
made the artist, her brush,
her colors so lush,
and ideas to paint from the heart.

He made the potter, the clay,
the writer of plays,
and all of the things we call art.

These are just some
of the things he has done
that make me shout out,
"I know God!"

27

I know God
made the music, the notes,
and the song in the throats
of the singers as they take the stage.

He gave them talent and flair
and gifts to spare
and excitement that jumps off the page.

These are just some
of the things he has done
that make me shout out,
"I know God!"

I know God
made me and made you
and him and her, too.
He made us all different and same.

He gave us hope, joy, and love
and help from above
whenever we call on his name.

These are just some
of the things he has done
that make me shout out,
"I know God!"

I Know God

Life Issue: I want my children to know God through his wonderful creation.
Spiritual Building Block: Faith

Use the following activities to help your children increase their awareness of God.

Sight:

Using whatever environment you are in (the car, the living room, outdoors), ask your children to name all the things they see that God made. As you talk about each of these things, point out how only God could make something that magnificent—for example, the simple sight a bird flying. Even though people can make many things, we can't make anything as wonderful and intricate as a flying bird.

Sound:

Read to your child Psalm 46:10, on which *I Know God* is based: "Be still and know that I am God." Ask your children to be still and listen. Then ask them to tell you what they heard and how they can know God better by the things they hear. Even a hungry, grumbling stomach speaks of God's amazing creation. Read another Bible verse to your children and talk about how we can know God even better through listening to his Word.

Touch:

Play the "I Know God" game (a variation of "I Spy"). Each person takes a turn finding something that God has made that is within reach and saying, "I know God because of something I can touch that is ____," and giving a brief description of the color and size. The others must guess what it is. After the game, tell the story of how God showed his love for us through Jesus' sacrifice on the cross.